JONNY ZUCKER began his career in radio and is now a writer and primary school teacher. Along the way he has played in several bands and has worked as a stand-up comedian. Jonny has written two books for adults: *A Class Act* and *Dream Decoder*. He lives in London with his wife and their young son.

JAN BARGER COHEN, originally from Arkansas in the U.S.A., is a well-established illustrator of children's books. Her previous titles include *Bible Stories for the Very Young*, the Little Animals series, *Incy Wincy Moo-Cow*, *Who Can Fly?*, *Who Can Jump?*, *Who Eats This?* and *Who Lives Here?*. She lives in East Sussex with her husband and a cocker spaniel called Tosca.

For Talia and Joseph – J.Z.
To Geoffrey and Audrey – J.B.C.

Eight Candles to Light copyright © Frances Lincoln Limited 2002
Text copyright © Jonny Zucker 2002
Illustrations copyright © Jan Barger Cohen 2002

First published in Great Britain in 2002 by
Frances Lincoln Limited, 4 Torriano Mews,
Torriano Avenue, London NW5 2RZ

www.franceslincoln.com

First paperback edition 2003

British Library Cataloguing in Publication Data available on request

ISBN 0-7112-2017-4

Printed in Singapore

3 5 7 9 8 6 4 2

FESTIVAL TIME!

Eight Candles to Light

A Chanukah Story

Jonny Zucker

Illustrated by Jan Barger Cohen

FRANCES LINCOLN

It's Chanukah. On the first
night we light one candle.
We listen to the amazing
story of Judah the Macabee.

We fry latkes in oil. They sizzle and spit in the pan! These potato cakes taste so good!

I love playing spinning games with a dreidel.

We sing songs about the brave Macabees and the cruel King Antiochus.

We all give each other presents
in colourful wrappings.

My family sits around the table
and enjoys a celebration meal.

We light eight candles to remind us of the miracle of Chanukah – our festival of light.

The Story Of Chanukah

About 2,100 years ago, the Greek king Antiochus wanted to make the Jews worship many gods, like all the other people in his empire. The Jews refused to pray to any but their one true God. Antiochus punished them by taking over the Holy Temple and destroying their sacred scrolls of the Law (the **Torah**). Many Jews were killed for refusing to bow down to the Greek gods.

In Modi'in, a town between Jerusalem and the sea, lived a Jewish priest called Mattathias with his five sons. When a Greek official tried to force the Jewish people to worship the Greek gods, Mattathias refused and killed the official. He and his sons and many other Jewish families fled to the hills, where they could hide from Antiochus' soldiers and fight against them.

Led by Mattathias' eldest son, Judah the Macabee, the Jews fought for three years and defeated Antiochus' army. They then returned to the Temple in Jerusalem. They wanted to relight the sacred **menorah** – the seven-branched candlestick – but there was only enough oil to keep it alight for one day, and they knew it would take eight days to get more oil. But a miracle happened: the oil kept burning for eight days and nights.

In memory of the miracle and the victory, Jewish people today light an eight-branched **menorah** at Chanukah-time.

One extra candle – the **shamash** or helper – is used to light the others. One candle is lit on the first evening, two on the second evening, until the eighth evening when eight candles are lit. These candles remind everyone how the oil in the Temple lasted for eight days.

During the festival, Jewish people sing special songs and give each other money and presents. To remind them of the miracle of the oil, they also eat doughnuts and **latkes** (potato cakes), which are fried in oil.

Children play games with spinning tops called **dreidels**. Each of the four faces of a **dreidel** has a Hebrew letter: **nun, gimmel, hey and shin**. When put together, they represent the phrase:

Nes gadol hayah sham – a great miracle happened there.

MORE TITLES IN THE FESTIVAL TIME! SERIES BY JONNY ZUCKER

Apples and Honey – A Rosh Hashanah Story
See how a Jewish family celebrates
New Year with this delightful book!
ISBN 0-7112-2016-6

Four Special Questions – A Passover Story
Read about matzah, the Seder plate, the four
questions and the hunt for the Afikoman.
ISBN 0-7112-2018-2

It's Party Time! – A Purim Story
A story about how a family celebrates Purim:
dressing up in costume, giving presents
and making lots of noise!
ISBN 0-7112-2019-0

Frances Lincoln titles are available from all good bookshops.
You can also buy books and find out more about your favourite titles,
authors and illustrators at our website: www.franceslincoln.com.